I0411319

Two free bonus books are included (making this book an $20.85 value!) Your books are presented in this order:

1) Spanked Before, During & After Sex: The Life of a Spanked Callgirl
2) The Absolutely Essential Guide to Great BDSM and S&M Sex
3) 100 Great Lines to Put In Your Personal Ads

Spanked Before, During & After Sex: The Life of a Spanked Callgirl

By Jenny Eller
Copyright (C) 2013

Chapter One

I am spanked professionally. Over the years I developed the ability to take amazingly long, hard spankings.

My father spanked me until I was 21. He gave me a choice of punishments and I invariably took the spanking. I was always able to take a hard spanking. When he stopped spanking me I knew I would need to find someone that would. For some reason I respect authority more if they spank me, and that includes my boyfriends and now my masters.

My butt doesn't bruise easily and I take pride in the number of paddles that have been broken over it. Perhaps my ass just doesn't have as many nerve endings as most folk's butts do.

I remember spitefully holding back my tears when being spanked as a child. I look back on that now and realize it was a mistake. I should have faked pain instead of having to deal with the alternative punishments they started giving me.

When I became an adult by chance I gravitated into the BDSM lifestyle as a masochist submissive. Well long story short. I lost my job in the other city I lived in, followed my master to this city but later found myself alone and broke. One night while sulking on the bed with only 2 weeks paid on the rent and $45 to my name, I hit on the idea to offer my services as a call girl that can be spanked.

I had seen so many professional spankee models' pictures in magazines and on the internet. Many were semi or completely naked while being spanked. I'd be just a professional spanking model if they didn't want sex. It would save them some money that way.

I would find clients that wanted to spank me for money, perhaps to help them with their own curiosity, pent-up frustrations, anger management, their desire to punish a female, need for stress relief, to relieve addictions, their desire for moral forgiveness and/or just for sexual stimulation. I had heard of spanking models offering private play sessions where they were spanked for a fee. As long as sex is not provided then hopefully it would be legal and if sex was requested well then sex it would be.

As I told you I was into BDSM and had established contacts here. I had been to play parties and had wowed others with my ability to be spanked. Fortunately I had made friends with a particularly popular master there. I got a hold of his phone number and gave him a call. That call would change my life. I start now from that next day.

I explained to Master Joe what I wanted to do and he said he could help for sure but first wanted me to play with him as a slave. I was not surprised, I was pretty, had a nice body and I knew he wanted to see what I could take. Frankly I needed a good hard play session anyway so I drove over to his house later that day.

Master Joe was himself quite good looking. "Come kneel in front of me young lady" he said glad to see me. I walked over to him with my eyes down. He was sitting on a couch. "Kneel". I knelt in front of him and close to him with my hands behind my head. He removed my top and bra and caressed and played with my tits. "Up higher on your knees young lady" he ordered. My breasts were now at his mouth level and he began sucking away on them. I was already so horny. He pulled both nipples into his mouth and sucked on them. My knees buckled from the pleasure. I don't think it was an orgasm but I continued begging for permission to cum, no such luck.

Master Joe then released my tits and pulled me towards him by the back of my head to kiss him. He stood up and removed his clothing. He then leaned back on the couch, spread his legs and ordered me to suck on his cock.

I had been taught that when I am eating a woman or sucking on a cock, I am to stick my butt up and out so it can be enjoyed and otherwise used by others behind me. Also with it up and out, by using long implements, my ass can be beaten by the person I'm pleasuring. I hadn't seen it when I had originally come over but next to him, Master Joe had already put his long red flogger. I leaned over to Master' cock and sucked on it. I really could suck on cock well, and for a long time. "Harder slave" I heard him say as he rested the flogger on my back. I lapped down Master' ooze, as I licked and sucked. This Master really took care of himself. He ate well, worked out, didn't smoke, etc and I could tell by how good his ooze tasted. I love good tasting ooze and I drank it down eagerly. Suddenly he began flogging my upturned ass cheeks as I sucked.   FLOP,   FLACK...SMACK,   CRACK...CRACK, BAM...FLOP, SMACK. The flogger kept landing mostly on my butt but also he flogged my back. He wasn't beating me particularly hard, besides I didn't care because I loved sucking on his cock and the beating was just getting me hornier.

Suddenly it stopped. "Head up young lady." I forced myself to stop sucking and took my head away from his wonderful cock. I kept my eyes on it hoping that being away from it would be just a temporary thing but it was not to be. "I need to see how well your tits deal with being whipped. I've seen you get spanked before but I'll also need to test how well your ass takes a beating too. "Yes Sir." "We'll start with the spanking and then I'll give you the tit whipping. I'm going to love to whip those gorgeous tits of yours." "Yes Master." "Give me your hands." I clapped my hands together on his lap and he tied them securely together. He motioned me to lay over his lap which I did. He began rubbing my butt. "Legs spread". I spread my legs about 2 feet wide. He then stuck his finger up my pussy. Wow did it ever easily slide in. "Wow, you are one wet slave girl. Very good. But no you're not cumming yet."

Master started my spanking with his hand. He went right to work too, *SMACK, BAM, slap, slap, BAM, slap.* I lost count as to how many spanks. Now he was spanking hard, smiling down on me as I squirmed, moaned and cried out. BAM, SPANK, SPANK, BAM, CRACK. I kicked my legs a bit. He was really laying it on fast and furious. Then suddenly I found myself on the verge of cumming. I knew Master wouldn't let me cum so why ask. I continued to yelp, moan and squirm. Suddenly I started cumming even though I didn't mean to. I tried hard not to move my pelvis in a manner that would give away that I was cumming without permission but suddenly Master' hard spanks meant a lot less. Then Master Joe stopped using his hand, reached for a strap and continued the deluge on my ass, rubbing it periodically to admire his work. I had a nice controlled orgasm as he spanked me. *SMACK, BAM...BAM, slap, slap, BAM, SMACK, slap.* I turned back to look at my ass and it was red. "Eyes forward" Master scowled giving me 5 really hard strokes to punctuate it. The spanking now was really hurting and as I had lost concentration, I also lost my orgasm, now all I felt was a lot of pain. *"Ow, noo Master, stop, oow, ow."* I pounded the couch in pain. He was really spanking hard. "Hold your ass still slave." I hadn't realized it but I had lifted my butt up some to avoid the spanks. Wow, that was a bad idea. Master went back to beating my ass and upper legs, this time with a medium size rubber paddle. "Ow, ooh, ooh, pleassee sir, I'llll be good." Dozens of spanks later I was crying. I can take a really hard spanking but all this attention to my posterior was really getting to me. Then suddenly it stopped.

"Kneel" was the order and I eagerly knelt in front of him as I rubbed my butt cheeks. Master bent over me and rubbed my hot butt cheeks. "This is a good test of what you can take." "Yes sir" I moaned. "Now it's time to give those lovely tits of yours the same kind of attention." Oh great, but at least my butt would get a rest for a change.

I had been trained to easily cum from breast stimulation. I am so proud of my breasts. They have given me and others so much pleasure. They can take quite a beating too. Master Joe specialized in tit torture so I suspect my tits would be red soon.

As I knelt in front of him, Master Joe untied my wrists and ordered me to turn around and put my wrists behind my back. He tied my hands behind my back and then ordered me to face him again. He then tied my boobs fairly tightly together at their base. My tits were even firmer than usual now. Their nipples quickly hardened. Master pinched both nipples hard waking me from my dreamy state and making me cry out.

Master then took out a short tit flogger and proceeded to lightly whip my tits with it as I continued to kneel in front of him. I closed my eyes instinctively but the flogger never came anywhere close to my face. Master Joe really knew how to whip tits. Master started to swing from a further distance away thus increasing the velocity. I could tell this was something he really enjoyed doing. This flogging went on for about 5 minutes. Master then put the flogger down and ordered me to turn around, my back now facing him, He now took up the same slapper he had earlier used on my butt. He pulled my head back by the hair exposing my breasts more and proceeded to spank them for real. *Slap, slap, slap, slap, slap, slap, slap.* Master concentrated spanking the fleshing mounds of the left breast, reaching out, grabbing it by the nipple and separating it from the right breast so more off my large breast was free to spank. It did sting but also felt sinfully good. *Smack...slap, slap, slap, BAM, slap.* Master pinched my left nipple as he held it making me wince but then he twisted it in-between his fingers giving me pleasure. He probably didn't even realize he was playing with the nipple in such a pleasurable way. Giving breasts pleasure and pain is just his nature. I sure wasn't going to complain. Then he let go of my left nipple and got a hold of the right nipple, pulling the right breast out to the right, separating it from its twin, allowing more of it to be beaten. Slap, slap, slap, slap, slap. Blow after blow continued to rain down on my breasts, making them pink and tender. Master pulled up my right breast by the nipple and concentrated his beating on the underside. It did hurt but frankly I was getting more pleasure from a tit whipping from him than when he spanked my ass. I glanced down at my breasts and they were getting red. Suddenly I blurted it out "Master please may I cum?"The whipping stopped suddenly as Master looked at me somewhat puzzled. "Wow, I love how masochistic you are." He them grabbed both of my large nipples together with one hand and pulled my breasts up exposing their soft underbelly, going to work on them both at once with the slapper and spanking them hard now. *"Ow, ohh no Master, ow, oww, oh pleeaaseee Master."* Slap...slap, slap...slap, slap. He let go of my tits. He then proceeded to spank their upper front. "Folks are going to love whipping your tits" "Yes Master." This was

6

hurting now and I wasn't going to be allowed to cum so I was going to just have to take it.

My breasts were now a shade of red and Master Joe stopped. I thought my tit whipping was over but I was wrong. "Turn around slave." I turned around obediently and knelt there as he untied my wrists. Then in my stupor I remembered that there was another position for me and my tits to be whipped in…and more.

Master, himself now naked, lead me over to the half table and ordered me to climb on it and lay on my back. The half table is many feet long with long vertical brackets so my upturn legs are kept in place securely. My arms and waist are strapped down to the table. My d-cup breasts thus are fully exposed and securely in place should they be the focus of attention, as they often are. On the half table my pussy and asshole are right on the edge of the table so they can be played with and taken with ease. My former master put me in one of these half tables at a friend's house often and left me there for his and sometimes other's pleasure. With my legs in this position I can easily be spanked and taken both in my pussy and ass.

Master tied each leg to the table's built-in leg braces. A strap came over my waist to keep it in place and straps held each wrist and upper arm in place. I was now quite vulnerable and immobile. I was also blindfolded. But for the time being Master Joe was a lot more interested in finishing the job he started with my breasts. Now though he would use the big black flogger to beat them.

Master bent down to my pussy and sucked the copious amount of cum out of it. "You know what's coming now young lady don't you." "Yes sir" I think I said. He raised the flogger and CRACK. "Ow". CRACK, CRACK…SMACK. This is a big room so Master could raise up the big flogger and let it fly. CRACK, CRACK…SMACK, BAM…SMACK, BAM. I was trying to move away but to no avail. I was held too tightly in place and could go nowhere. BAM, SMACK, BAM. Master was working up a sweat and loving every second of it. I was so exposed and I knew by now my pussy was dripping wet. I couldn't wait for him to take me. Hopefully he'll take me for a long time too. I held onto that thought as the blows rained down on my chest. *"Master, please, ohh, ahhh."* Master was very skilled and the flogger never landed more than a couple of inches above my breasts. Finally it was over.

He now played with my sensitive breasts grabbing, kneading, twisting, turning and holding them. "I am so proud of my work and your breasts are so much fun to work with. People are going to pay good money to beat you." Well I guess that's good. I had bills. "Thank you master." I muttered. Master bent down and lightly bite my nipples one by one, also sucking on them and playing with my breasts more. He clearly loved my tits. Suddenly I remembered what could come next, yes, it could be the highlight of my day.

I looked down at my chest and it was a red. My nipples were hot and sensitive. I heard Master doing something and I looked over at him. He had made himself hard and was coming over to my exposed holes. First he got out some Vaseline and used his finger to lubricate my anus. He inserted his finger deep into it making me moan in anticipation. He then cleaned off his finger with alcohol and a paper towel. "Beg for it slave" he ordered. "Master please take me." "You can do better than that." "Master I'm begging, please take me and fuck me hard." Then he entered my pussy. Immediately I began begging to cum, which he allowed me to do.

Master grabbed my upper legs to hold me in place while he pounded my pussy. I came so hard. I lost track of what time it was. "Come harder slut" he roared and I did just that pumping my hips against him as he took me. I couldn't wait for him to take me in my ass. "You like how this feels in that naughty little cunt of yours don't you slave." "Yes sir" I stammered. He pounded me harder and buried his cock in my pussy, just leaving it there for a few moments as he gyrated his hips, making his cock move from side to side. I was so wet that it slide easily in my pussy. "Wow, you're one soaking wet little slave girl." I couldn't answer though I think I tried. I was cumming so hard. About then he pulled out of my pussy and stuck his cock in my ass. *"Ohhhhh Master, yes, thank you....ohhh."* He started taking me slowly in the ass at first but built up speed and after a couple of minutes was pounding my butthole with vigor. I felt no pain, just waves of ecstasy.

Master finished taking me a while later and cleaned off his equipment as I lay tied down exhausted and helpless. He left me there with my spread legs up in the air. My tits a shade of red and my ass somewhat sore and tender. He went to the couch and we talked about my being a professional spankee.

Master Joe was impressed by how much abuse my body could take and was confident I could make a decent living doing this. I didn't bruise that much which would be helpful. It was important though that I don't have sex if I took money. Amazingly he actually thought that as long as sexual favors were not offered, the law was more on my side if a client tried to abuse me. Of course if the police were called I would now be in their sights which would not be to my benefit.

For the next hour he kept me tied to the half table checking to see how my body dealt with the beatings. He also took the opportunity to take me again before releasing me. In exchange for regularly being his sex slave, he promised to help me and even said he could get me 2 clients immediately. He even said he'd spread the word that I was a friend of his cousin, a city policeman.

Advice he gave was:

1. Use condoms
2. Avoid fellatio
3. Use an online phone number that would be difficult to trace
4. Get the cash up front
5. Don't use my real name.
6. Spankings could only be done using their hands, unless they pay extra
7. Ideally they need to be recommended to me by someone I trust.
8. Give my butt and/or tits enough time to heal in between clients.
9. Have a safe word and make sure they understand my limits
10. Tit whipping would cost extra.

Master Joe released me and we had something to eat on his porch. That would be the last time he would beat me for some time. However when I came over to be his sex toy, he loved seeing all the marks on my body and where it was red. He would be a comforting friend and lover during this busy period of my life.

Three days later I had a bruise-free ass and my first client.

Chapter Two

Master got me my first client, Dick. I knew him from a play party. I also knew he was a married, veteran spanker, thus knew how to spank. We agreed on the terms and a time that night and the price of $100. There would be no sex.

I drove over to his place. Unexpectedly Dick had a friend there, John. John had never spanked a girl before and was interested in it. As agreed I took the cash as I walked in and sat on the couch in his living room waiting for the inevitable spanking.

We first all had some wine. He then brought a wooden spanking horse out for me to bend over. It had straps for the spankee but Master Joe had previously made it plain that I don't allow myself to be strapped in, unless he was there, which he wasn't. I would first get spanked OTK by both of them and then get spanked over the wooden spanking horse.

The truth was that I didn't know what the definition of a full, complete spanking was and they wondered themselves. I told them that my butt can be red.

I was told to lay over Dick's lap, which I did. Dick raised my skirt and pulled my panties down and off. He massaged and kneaded my ass for some time as he talked to John. Wow, that massaging felt good. Then he started spanking. *Slap, slap, slap, BAM, slap, crack, slap, bam, slap, Bam.* This was a basic warm-up spanking which I was grateful for. Dick explained the importance of a warm up spanking to John but he added that it was for *when a girl was going to get spanked for some time.* Apparently he wanted to get his hundred dollar's worth. I gulped but I guess that's what they're supposed to be able to do to a professional callgirl spankee.

Spank, spank, slap, spank, slap, BAM, slap, crack, SMACK. I squirmed a bit and repositioned myself for a long stay over his lap. He spanked with a steady rhythm. *Spank, smack, smack, slap, smack.* I began softly moaning after the 20th spank and the noises I would make grew progressively louder from then on. He concentrated on the right cheek for some time, then the left cheek but my butt could outlast a lot of spankers and soon he was shifting from his tired right hand to his fresher left hand and then back to his right hand. *"Owww, ohh, ahhh."* Still the spanking went on and on and hurt! *SMACK, bam, bam, slap, slap, SMACK.* Then he stopped and I caught my breath. I hadn't started crying yet but was getting quite a charge from the spanking. He on the other hand was tired. How great was that. I still laid there over his lap and actually he continued to hold me firmly in place.

Dick called John over who brought a chair and sat across from him. I was now in-between them, lucky me. John then started spanking the cheek closest to him and Dick spanked the cheek closest to him. *Spank, SMACK, spank, SPANK, spank, spank, spank, crack, SMACK.* Should I be charging more for this duo spanking stuff?

"It's amazing how tough your butt is, all there is is some redness" said John, impressed. *Slap, spank, BAM, slap, crack, spank, bam.* John spanked down my upper leg and Dick told him to stay on my butt. *Spank, crack, spank, bam.* It was hurting significantly now *"Ahhh, ohhh, owww"* I said. The spanks landed 2-3 a second with both of them spanking me. *Spank, spank, spank, bam, slap, Bam.* I began kicking my feet up and down a foot or two, much to their delight. I know I also was giving them a great view of my anus and pussy as modesty was no longer a priority as my butt reddened.

My spanking had lasted about 30 minutes and I looked back and saw that my butt was red and somewhat marked. I was crying out with every spank now. A good spanking leaves the spankee with a red butt so I worked up the courage to say okay guys that that was enough. A minute or so later the spanking stopped.

I wanted to get up but Dick wanted to use his fingernails to rake my hot, red butt before massaging it for a while. I never thought of that but I would have to get used to that after the spanking stops. The raking of the butt didn't hurt as much as the actual spanking of course and after all admiring their work would be exciting for them and less painful for me than the actual spanking. I submissively kept on lying across his lap. Both massaged my butt and wow did it feel good but I knew where somebody's hand was going to go. "Please guys, only my butt, it stays legal that way." Well I hoped that was how it stayed legal anyway. John got to rake and massage the cheek he worked his magic on and Dick got to rake and massage the cheek he spent the most time on.

I put my hands back on the carpet and waited for them to be through. I guess for $100 they deserve to relax that way.

We made some small talk and John got my wine and brought it to me as I continued to lay over Dick's lap. I asked Dick if I could get up and he said no. Well it was $100 he spent so I laid there. Finally he had to go to the bathroom and my first spanking for money was over.

Fortunately I loved the feeling of a sensitive, sore well-spanked butt rubbing against my panties. Good thing because I would have a sore butt quite a bit from now on. I was grateful that my first spanking gig went well. Dick knew Master Joe and wanted to stay in good graces with this town's BDSM community. He was also a good guy. I could only hope I would be so lucky from now on with my clients.

Word of mouth is such a powerful business force. I had left cards with the guys and 3 days later I got a call from someone they knew.

His name was Tom and was a business associate of Master Joe's. He actually was in town for only a short time. We chatted on specifics and set a time for me to come over that night. Once again I would get a good, long spanking but sex would likely occur this time.

I met Tom at the hotel bar and we chatted. I was a good listener and I would find that was a real asset in this line of work. After a while we went up to his room. I went in to use the bathroom and came out and he was naked. He sat on the bed and I, still fully clothed, I laid over his lap.

No matter how many spankings I have gotten in life I still get butterflies in my stomach when I'm about to get another good one. I was now in my familiar position of lying over a man's lap, butt up, with my hands on the floor and feet hanging down the other end. The dress I had worn was a short, thin, sexy one. It's important to keep the client hungry for you as $150 is a good deal of money. He massaged my fully clothed butt, upper legs, tits and pussy apparently in no hurry to start the spanking. Then he pulled up my dress, massaging my panty-covered butt for a bit and then pulled my panties all the way off of me. Tom explained to me that he hadn't had sex in months since he separated from his girlfriend and was really looking forward to taking me after and during the spanking.

Tom's spanking started with more intensity than I expected. *Spank, spank, spank, slap, slap, crack.* My butt was no longer sore from the spanking several days ago so it needed a bit of breaking in again. Slap, crack, spank, spank, spank.*"Ohhhhhh"* I muttered unexpectedly as the spanking continued. He ordered me to give him my right hand and he held it firmly to my lower back making it tougher for me to move around. "Young lady I'm going to turn this lovely ass a very nice shade of red." *Spank, spank, spank, slap, bam.* "Oww, ohhhh." My feet started kicking as he picked up the pace of the spanking. Instinctively I squeezed my butt cheeks together and tightened them up. He seemed to spank harder when I did that though. *"Ahh, ohh."* "Do you think I'm capable of giving you a good spanking young lady" he asked clearly enjoying beating my ass. "Yes sir" I said in-between spanks. Wow, he could spank, he wasn't missing a beat, though he was switching off to his other hand periodically. *Spank, slap, slap, bam, BAM.* "Now we're getting somewhere. You're butt's getting red, but it's got a ways to go."

You just never know what the guy's going to become like when he's spanking. He was quite the gentleman down at the bar when we first met but now was a tiger, still I was getting spanked so what did I expect. *"Ow, ow, oh....oh...ow."* Well I had officially entered the serious pain zone. I looked back at my ass and he was right, it was getting red. I also realized I had become horny and now that I was kicking my feet with a bit more gusto, he could easily see my anus and pussy. I tried to close my legs but the spanking was too intense. He unexpectedly stopped spanking but he wasn't letting me up. I quickly tried to get up but was held down. 'No young lady, this spanking is not over. You lay still" he said very firmly. I wanted to say that that was enough of a spanking but he was so firm with me that I was scared to. I waited for the inevitable to continue. He rubbed my red ass all the way down my legs. He then played with my wet pussy which was a welcome sensation. After a while I was ordered to get up and remove my remaining cloths. At least the spanking had stopped. I slowly got up and braced myself on one of his shoulders as I took off the rest of my clothing. He wanted me to suck on this cock but I said I couldn't, but I would use my hand on him. I reached for the lotion to put on his cock but he ordered me to only use my hand. It was a good idea since the lubricant, even dried off, could still make the condom slip off when he took me later.

I had been trained to always massage a man's balls when sucking on, or playing with his cock. This time was no different. I also knew that if I got him to cum, he might become less interested in spanking me. Unfortunately he knew that too and ordered me to slow down the speed of my masturbating him. He reached down and played with both my breasts as I played with him. His hands felt good and I started to really slow down the tempo of my masturbating his penis. I was looking at his penis and didn't realize that he had picked up a strap. He spanked me 5 quick hard times with it and ordered me to do a better job with his cock. I quickly came too and complied. Fortunately he went back to playing with both my tits.

5 or 10 minutes of this went by and it was once again time for the rest of my spanking. Naked, I laid back down over his lap as ordered.

He raked my sore ass with his fingernails. It all had been a very nice break but the problem was his spanking muscles had gotten recharged for round 2…and then along came round two and now he was really spanking hard. *SPANK, SPANK, Spank, spank,*

spank, slap, BAM. I kicked my legs as my now sensitive red cheeks bounced up and down from the blows. I pushed up on his leg with my free hand as I tried feebly to get away but he held me too tight. The blows rained down on my exposed ass. I cried out with each blow. He was really going for it. *"Ow, owwwww...ohhh...oww."* SPANK SPANK, SPANK, spank, spank, BAM, BAM. Then suddenly he stopped. He was breathing hard and my ass really hurt.

He just looked down at me, massaging my hot, red ass and wet pussy. Then he raked both cheeks again with his dull but significant sized fingernails. That caught me off guard. I caught my breath. I felt the cool air in the hotel room on my ass. I wasn't sure who was going to speak first. Finally I spoke. "That was really quite a spanking." I suddenly realized though that he had a very tight grip on me and I wasn't going to be able to get up unless he let go of me. "May I get up now SIR" I said. As if in a trance he suddenly came to and released me. I slipped off his lap and came to rest on my knees on the carpet below him, immediately vigorously rubbing my sore butt. I would have been a nice sight as he looked down at me. I was instinctively looking at his cock, I really wanted to suck on it but I knew that was too risky in my line of work. He just sat there looking down at me. His cock was hard and staring at me.

I was ordered onto the double bed and on my hands and knees. I complied. I put the condom behind me and waited to be taken. He climbed on the bed, put the condom on and entered my pussy. Oh did I ever need this. "You have a nice tight pussy". I work hard to make it as tight as possible I told him. A tight pussy comes in handy in my line of work.

I had talked to Master Joe about it previously and it was decided that I didn't need permission to cum when in these sex situations while working. That worked fine with me and within 20 seconds my orgasm started and within 5 minutes so did his and that was that.

16

I gingerly sat down across from him on the double bed and we talked. He was actually a neat guy to talk to. I congratulated him on really getting his money's worth as I fidgeted while sitting. Soon I left his room, that much closer to paying rent.

That next day I called Master Joe to thank him for the contact and ask him when he next wanted me to come over and serve him. Happily he said in an hour and gave me instructions on what to wear and what to do.

I got there in the skirt and blouse he ordered me to wear. I wasn't allowed to wear underwear but thankfully could wear a bra as the blouse he wanted me to wear was somewhat see-through. I let myself in as instructed and immediately went and kneeled in front of him. We talked for a while as he undressed me. He then had me lay over his lap so he could inspect my ass. It was still marked and a little red from last night's spanking. It was firmer too. My butt gets firm from being well spanked. He was really impressed and would later call Tom and congratulate him on a job well done. He massaged my ass and teased my pussy for a bit with a vibrator but sadly wouldn't let me cum.

Master would have loved to have tied me up naked and beaten me, and frankly other than on the butt, I wouldn't have minded either but I had to be as mark-free as possible. He did however still have a lot he could do with my body. I was ordered to put my hands behind the small of my back and he tied them together. I then was ordered to sit in front of him so his chest was against my back. He then commenced playing with my breasts. It felt so good. I started to say something but he ordered me to be silent. He then took out a bottle of massage oil, put big globs on both his hands and commenced to massage my breasts using the lubrication of the massage oil. Within 20 seconds I was ready to cum. I asked for permission and got it. *"Ahhhhh, yes, ohhhhhhhhhh."* As my hands were tied behind my back, and I was up against Master, I was able to play with his cock and instinctively I did. He wasn't real hard but soon would be. Using his hands, Master Joe ran circles around the lubricated fleshy part of my breasts for many minutes making me beg to have my nipples played with. *"Master Joe please play with my nipples so I can cum harder for you."* That was the way to ask a Master as he suddenly did and my body shook from the intenseness of the orgasm. *"Awwwwwww yessssss, awwwwww."* Waves of pleasure rolled over me and I strained at my bonds as the spasms engulfed me. *"Awwwwww."* 20 minutes of this came and went and like all good things, it ended. But what a divine interlude it was.

Then he then ordered me to turn around and slide down to his cock and put my mouth to good use.

It's a good thing I have such a strong mouth as Master had me sucking for a long time. He came and I remained there with his cock in my mouth for around 10 minutes to make sure to drink up all of his cum.

After that he took me to his bedroom and I massaged him for around an hour. He then decided he would take me after-all.

I was ordered to go to the half-table, the table I was strapped down to and taken last time I was here. Thank goodness. I really wanted him to take me.

As previously noted, the half table is many feet long with braces so my legs are kept up and in place securely. My arms and waist are strapped down to the table. My breasts are fully exposed and securely in place. On the half table my pussy and asshole are right on the edge of the table so they can be played with and taken with ease. With my legs in this position I can easily be taken both in my pussy and ass.

Master tied each leg to the table's built-in stirrups. A strap came over my waist to keep it in place and straps held each wrist and upper arm in place. I was now quite vulnerable and immobile. I was also blindfolded.

Master came over and entered my pussy.

Master grabbed my upper legs to hold me in place while he pounded my pussy with his cock. I came so hard. "Come harder slave" he roared and I did just that. I couldn't wait for him to take me in my ass. He pounded me harder and buried his cock in my pussy, just leaving it there for a few seconds. I was cumming so hard. A few minutes later he pulled out of my pussy and stuck his cock in my ass. *"Ohhhhh Master, yes, thank you....ahhh."* He started taking me slowly in the ass at first but built up speed and after a couple of minutes was pounding my ass with vigor. I felt no pain, just pleasure.

Master finished taking me a while later and left me tied down exhausted and helpless. He left me there with my spread legs up in the air and went about his business. I dozed off.

Chapter Three

I got a call from Master a few days later. He had a couple of guys that wanted to only spank me and would pay $200 but insisted on using implements. He said I would be spanked really hard. They would do it at his place. I would spend a lot of the spanking tied up naked to the half table. I was reluctant to say no to any of his requests so I agreed. It would happen that night and I should be wearing a schoolgirl outfit when I got there.

I knew this would be a real hard spanking that would make me cry hard. It made me scared and I had butterflies in my stomach for the rest of the day. It was as if I knew I was going to be punished later by a parent or master and really wished it could be over with already. My marks from the previous spanking had gone so at least they would start with a fresh ass, something no doubt they'd like. The truth is that I loved being strapped down to the half table and at least Master would be there to watch things.

I got there in my schoolgirl outfit looking very cute. I had put my hair in pigtails, something I hadn't done in a while. The guys were there and I nervously looked at them. Sadly they looked pretty strong, but at least they were good looking.

I sat down on a chair between Tim and Frank. Master brought me a glass of wine. We chatted. They seemed pretty nice but I know how guys can get when they start spanking, they become animals. They wanted to see my butt so I took off my skimpy panties and backed to one, then the other, lifting up my schoolgirl skirt when I got to each. They enjoyed feeling it, massaging it, kneading it and I stayed in front of each until they told me they were done. I told them that I had had butterflies in my stomach all day anticipating this.

"Your ass is a perfect ass for spanking" one said. Oh lucky me.

I'd been there for about 30 minutes and Master came over and sat on the couch. Sternly he ordered me to strip, which I did. My nipples were already erect knowing what was to come.

I stood before them naked. I then was ordered to go over to Master who tied my hands together in front of me. I then told the guys that I expected to cry from this and that it was okay.

What was to come was one of the longest and hardest spankings I've ever had.

I was instructed to lie over Frank's lap which I did. Frank didn't waste any time and got right into spanking me. Oh did I forget to mention that he had big hands? *SPANK, spank, bam, bam, spank, slap, spank.* I hunkered down to be soundly beaten. *Bam, bam, spank, slap.* I tried not to raise my feet this early in the spanking and kept thinking about the $200 I would make from this. Rent and utilities would be paid for this month and just in the nick of time too. Then frank gave me 5 of his hardest and it made me yell out. "Ahhhhhhh." They all had a laugh. "Ow that hurt" I said more for the fun of it than anything. Frank rubbed my butt again for a bit and got back to the spanking. *Slap, SMACK, slap, SMACK, slap, BAM, slap, crack, SMACK. "Ohhhh.......ahhhh"*. He was spanking harder now and really enjoying himself. I sucked in air and clenched my fingers as serious pain had officially kicked in. If only I could cum from it. I needed to try and cum. It would make the spanking a lot more enjoyable. I tried rubbing his leg inconspicuously then he hit me with those 5 super hard ones again. BAM, BAM, BAM, BAM, BAM. *"Ahhhhh, owwww."* I was now always crying out from the spanking. Then it stopped. Frank rubbed my butt, also grabbing handfuls of butt cheek which hurt actually. He was pleased with his work but fair is fair and it was Tim's turn for me to lay over his lap and be spanked. I was ordered to get up and lay over Tim's lap. Oh that felt great, not only had the spanking stopped for precious seconds but I got to move my butt, but with my hands tied in front of me I couldn't rub it. I slowly walked over to Tim who ordered me to "hurry up". I laid over his lap and, well here we go again.

Tim spanked in a hold different way. I don't think he had done much if any spanking before. The good news is that he wasn't spanking hard. He spanked all over my butt, top left cheek, then next spank was bottom right cheek, then the middle of a cheek, etc.

It was kind of neat actually. "So what does my butt look like?" I asked for the fun of it now that I wasn't crying out in pain from every spank. "Red; it's a nice start anyway" Tim said reminding me that the festivities of the night were just starting and my butt was the main event. Spank, spank, spank, slap, BAM, slap, crack, SMACK. "O*www.*" I scrunched my toes and now made regular yelps as he really was spanking hard now.

Before I knew it around 10 minutes had passed and I now was crying. I was then ordered to get up off of Tim's lap. I so wanted to rub my now bruised well spanked butt and didn't care that I was naked and everybody was gazing at my full frontal nudity. Of course I couldn't as I my hands were tied in front of me. "Does it hurt young lady?" Frank asked sarcastically. "Yes sir" I quickly answered. They smiled. Then the guys started walking towards the half table. Master was already there. "Get on the table young lady" Master said and I grudgingly started walking over there. As I walked by Frank though he put his arm out across my stomach so I was kept checked in place while he ran his other hand over my ass. "Nice warm ass". He let me go and I walked over to the half table, climbed on and lay on my back. My upturned legs were put in the leg braces and held securely in place with straps. My hands were untied and then my arms and waist were strapped down to the table. I was also blindfolded. On the half table my ass was right on the edge of the table so it can be beaten with ease. Then much to my surprise, Master brought over a ball gag and gagged me. I knew Master had a sadistic streak in him and it then dawned on me how he was really going to enjoy seeing me get beaten like this. I hadn't counted on being gagged but too late now.

I don't know who was doing it but both ass cheeks were getting raked, rubbed, pinched and kneaded. Then someone put a vibrator on my pussy and ordered me to cum, which I gladly did. Somehow these guys seemed to into beating me to let me have that much pleasure and sure enough the vibrator was gone in less than a few minutes, still that was a very welcome interlude.

Oh god, the spanking is about to start again, I just know it. CRACK. Oh no, both of them had a strap and were staggering their swats. One gave me a spank from one side and the other gave me a swat from the other side. The first blow landed smack down the middle of both cheeks. It was a wonderfully aimed spank I must admit but hurt so much. I lurched all I could being strapped down so tight. My constant yells were muffled by the gag. The strapping though continued and it hurt something fierce. CRACK, CRACK, CRACK, CRACK, BAM, BAM. My ass and now upper legs were being beaten by the straps, and non-stop. The sound the strap made when it landed on my ass reverberated through the room. CRACK, CRACK, CRACK. It could be my worst beating in months. SMACK, BAM, BAM...SMACK, SMACK, BAM. I bet all my muffled crying was making their cocks hard. Someone grabbed my legs and lifted my ass higher exposing more ass to spank. The strapping continued. SMACK, SMACK, SMACK, BAM, BAM, BAM, BAM. I tried to move my ass but it was too securely in place. My ass was pulled out and up as far as the pelvic strap would allow all in an effort to expose as much ass as possible. SMACK, SMACK, SMACK, BAM, BAM. Frank and Tim were in heaven, they could now really beat a slave girl like they had always dreamed of. I could not escape the blows that were raining down on my ass. Tears were running down my cheeks. I can usually take a good beating but as sensitive as my ass was already and with such a beating on my tender ass with straps, was too much. I know this spanking will leave so many marks on my ass and I didn't expect to be able to sit.

The spanking stopped. I so hoped it had ended. My ass still was on fire. I felt cold hands massaging it as I kept crying from the lingering pain. I pulled on my wrist straps. I was ready for this to end but the blindfold and gag held. What I didn't know is that the two guys had exchanged their straps for paddles and the deluge on my ass would now once again begin. *SMACK, CRACK, SPANK, SPANK, SPANK.* I was already crying so I now just cried harder. I clenched my butt cheeks but doing just that really hurt and then there were the blows raining down on my clenched cheeks. Also it was now difficult to think of anything but the pain. Oh god if there was something they wanted me to stop doing I promise I will. I'll be such a good girl. SPANK, SPANK...SMACK, SPANK, SPANK. I heard them talking but I couldn't make out what they said. They were stopping now more often and rubbing my butt in-between swats and occasionally adjusting my blindfold to make sure it covered my eyes completely. After around 15 minutes more of off and on paddling, it stopped. I remained strapped down helpless. I also remained crying. After more massaging of my butt the voices became more distant. Was it over yet? I also became aware of wetness running down my ass crack. I had become so wet that that it was running down from my pussy. No doubt that was an exciting sight for everybody.

Then they came back and this time each took a turn individually with the paddle. I couldn't believe it. I just kept crying. What else could I do? I'm so glad the ball gag was on me because all my crying had become embarrassing. In time the spanking ended but my crying continued. My ass was so sore.

I remained strapped down to the half table. Soon though I didn't hear the guy's voices and I knew the spanking had ended. I tried hard and finally was able to stop crying. I remained strapped down to the half table whimpering on and off. I was exhausted. I figured Master would let me up soon which was a saving grace. I think I even fell asleep.

I was awoken by a mouth sucking on my pussy, drinking up my cum. I had to assume it was Master. The ball gag was still on me as well as the blindfold. My ears were actually ringing. I didn't know why. Then the pussy eating got really intense. Magically a vibrator appeared and I came so hard. I forgot about my intense beating and so incredibly sore ass and shook with such an intense orgasm. Master ran the vibrator along my clit then entered me while massaging me with the vibrator. Oh man was that ever intense. I don't know where I found the energy but I had such an uncontrollable orgasm. The truth is that I don't know when it ended because I passed out or fell asleep at some point.

When I woke up I noticed that I could see light. Not only was the blindfold off of me but I was also unstrapped, good thing because I had to go to the bathroom quick. I ran in and sat on the toilet and *owwwwww*. I forgot about my severely spanked ass. I would need to take care when sitting for a while. I climbed into bed with Master and that would be it for that wild night's experience.

I slept in the next day and was tired through much of it. Master and I had sex twice as both of us were really horny. Master invited some BDSM friends over to see my butt. It was a work of art and frankly I was very proud of it. He counted 14 bruises and even late that afternoon it was still reddish. People *ewwed and ahhed*. Nobody had ever seen a butt the next day that well spanked. That night Frank even came over to see his handiwork. I was kind of scared to see him actually but he promised it was just to look and not to spank. He too was really impressed and we took pictures that only showed my butt. I would later use those pictures to help get clients.

I went home the next day and continued to give my butt a well deserved rest.

Chapter Four

4 nights later I got a call from someone that nobody knew. As nobody knew him I decided against meeting him. He would call again though.

About a week later most of my bruises were gone and good thing as Master had a new client for me and he would become a regular.

We talked on the phone and I told him how he had to spank with his hand and other specifics. He agreed. Once again I would go to Master' house for it, which was my preference anyway. I had come to realize that Master really enjoyed watching others spank me and spank me hard. I guess the arrangement worked to my favor as I was safer there.

The truth was I hadn't been spanked in a week and I really needed it. I'm a spankophile and even after that extreme spanking I had, I remained addicted to being spanked. Frankly the lingering pain from that spanking made me horny. I kind of missed it. Obviously being a spankophile comes in handy if one is a professional spankee.

I got in a sexy dress, put on my make-up, got the high heels on and drove over to Master'. I hung out watching TV but Jim never showed up. He called an hour later and apologized and asked to re-schedule for tomorrow. Master added $40 for my wasted time and gasoline tonight and he agreed.

Come nightfall, I got all the sexy clothing back on and went back to Master' house, not sure he would even show up. He did, though he was 25 minutes late. He put the money on the TV, I took it and put it in my purse.

I really didn't know what to think of him. He wasn't shaved but didn't smell. Master gave him a drink, (oh that's another thing about getting spanked at Master's place, he throws in free drinks!) We talked about how I loved to be spanked and his spanking experience with adults and I guess he had plenty. Okay well so what now. He looked over at Master and asked how to proceed. That was nice of him. Master told me to strip and lay over his lap as he sat on the couch.

Just the thought of being spanked had made me wet and frankly I had been horny all day thinking about it. If he hadn't shown up tonight I would have begged Master for a spanking.

As I lay over his lap he commented about what a beautiful sight I was, which was nice. He then slid his hand down and cupped a boob. Soon the other hand was playing with my other boob. Nice. He ran his fingers over my nipples.

"Now which of these shall I use." He first picked up a black leather paddle but put it down instead opting for a ping pong paddle. He rubbed my butt tenderly with his hands for a while, then with the paddle. "I'll enjoy leaving my mark on your lovely ass."

Well the rubbing was fun while it lasted but then he started spanking in earnest. *SMACK... BAM, slap, slap...BAM, SMACK...SMACK, BAM...BAM, slap, slap, slap.* I started squirming. "Hold still slave or this spanking will never end." Gee, that didn't sound like fun. I quickly gained my composure and largely stayed put. SMACK, SMACK, slap, slap, BAM, SMACK, SMACK... BAM, slap. My butt by now was tender enough for me to really feel the swats. *"Ow, ow, no please, ow, aw, aw, stop please, oh."* "Music to my ears" he said as he started spanking me harder. "Oh please no, owww." I grabbed once again on to the couch cushion and held onto it with all my might. Fortunately my butt began acclimating to the blows and the pain tapered off some. Then he started with the irregular blows. I hate those. He'd rub my butt with the paddle then quickly raise it and bring it down on me, many times in rapid succession. *"Now let's see how fast I can give you 50".* I didn't just hear 50 did I? SMACK, BAM, slap, BAM, slap, slap, BAM, SMACK. I was squirming as the blows really hurt. I tried to stay in place as much as possible. I raised and lowered my butt some from the pain. RAT, TAT, TAT, BAM, BAM, SMACK, BAM. *"Stop pleasssssse sir, I'll be gooooodd."* 29, 30, 31, 32, he counted out. I started kicking my feet some but caught myself and held back as much as I could. I cried out as he started the 40s. He was now spanking with all his might. *"Ow, no sir, stop, oww, ow."* Abruptly he pushed me off his lap and dropped the paddle. I rubbed my scorching bottom.

He ordered me to bend over the seat of the couch. I crawled there so thankful the spanking was over. He took off his cloths and after putting a condom on, took me from behind as he reached down and played with my tits. Soon he came and soon he left. I however was ordered by master to stay in that position as he planned on taking me that way too, and indeed he did.

Well a few days later Jack called for the first time and left a message. Jack is a very nice senior citizen who was looking for an adult school girl to lecture and punish. I would drive to his place in a schoolgirl outfit or something girlish and act like a scared young lady. He would lecture me about something, give me a good spanking, though not too hard, and send me into the corner. Usually I would get 3 spankings in-between my corner time and being lectured. Due to his age perhaps he didn't seem to have a strong sex drive but he did take me sometimes. He would thankfully become a regular and I counted on him to spank me almost as often as I wanted. In fact I often called him up and asked him if he wanted a session with me. Sometimes he'd go to master' house to watch me get spanked by master (and even join in the fun.)

Regulars like Jack are the thing to have. I started specializing in bad schoolgirl fantasies for older men and always was able to pay my bills.

Well off to my next spanking. See ya!

This book is sold and/or distributed with the understanding that the publisher and author is not engaged in rendering legal or other professional services. **This book and its subject matter is for entertainment purposes only.** In this publication there may be inadvertent inaccuracies including technical inaccuracies, typographical inaccuracies and other possible inaccuracies. **The writer and publisher of this publication expressly disclaim all liability for the use or interpretation by anybody of information contained in this publication.** The author, publisher and distributors of this publication hereby disclaim any and all liability for any loss or damage caused by errors or omissions resulted from negligence, accident, or any other causes. If legal advice or other expert assistance is required, the services of a competent professional person in a consultation capacity should be sought. Products, services and websites' content vary with time. Please verify any published information.

The Absolutely Essential Guide to Great BDSM and S&M Sex

Copyright (C) 2013 by Phil G.

Let's Begin...

Just a quick bit of information about my lovemaking style, I am a sexually dominant, heterosexual. I need my lady love to be able to orgasm-on-demand, or agree to be trained for it. Typically she's trained to have extremely long orgasms versus several comparatively shorter ones. This is part of where my sexual dominance comes in. My lover will need to start her orgasm quickly, and continue it for as long as I am sexually stimulating her by using my hands or other parts of my body. Fortunately the human female body is built to have long, frequent and powerful orgasms, though so comparatively few women get to enjoy their incredible built-in capacity for pleasure. The truth is that orgasm-on-demand is a remarkably easy thing for women to do once properly trained.

Most men concentrate on a woman's body to stimulate her sexually, (which in and of itself is not a bad idea) but in so many cases that's not enough. I have found that most men do not adequately sexually stimulate their women's minds.

There is a natural tendency by women to be the more submissive sex during sexual activity, and that would certainly be required for the 3 hour playtime we're discussing. (Please note that if this tendency toward submissive behavior is not true in your case then this type of orgasm on demand training likely won't work too well with you.)

In her now sexually aroused state, it's normal for her subconscious mind to be more susceptible to suggestions regarding sex. People like me take it a step further and require her to do more than that during her sexual submission, specifically she will be required to orgasm long and hard, no ifs, ands or butts. Thus it is no longer her decision on how hard and long to orgasm but her lover's and I for one will require her to orgasm relentlessly.

Another way to look at it is that after being trained for orgasm on demand, the woman no longer is the one making the decision as to when *she* is going to have her orgasms and/or how intense the orgasm will be. She has yielded that responsibility to her lover and her mind fully accepts his/her authority in the matter.

Let's remember, a woman's subconscious mind doesn't usually care who tells it to begin orgasming, it can be her own mind giving the order or it can be her lover's. As a woman you just have to be in the right frame of mind to let it happen.

For 3 hours of sex it is very helpful if the man lasts a long time and/or is capable of getting hard frequently and with minimal downtime.

I last an extremely long time, usually for at least the whole 3 hours. I also have a thick penis which of course is a help.

Incidentally if someone is looking for an easy to find penis desensitizer cream, over the counter hemorrhoid cream under the tip of the penis can work well. I would urge the man to test it out on himself before being with a woman as if too much is used he might not even feel the stimulation enough to get hard! The man needs to know just the right amount to use and chances are it's a small amount.

I wanted to note that the dominant sexual position discussed in this book works best when the woman is no more than somewhat overweight.

Here are specifics of what we'd do in our 3 (or more) hour playtime.

1. When you enter my (our) place, you will take off your shoes and go kneel on the thick padding next to my bed (or other agreed upon spot like a chair or couch). Unless told otherwise, your eyes will be looking at where my midsection would be when I sit down in front of you. You will wait for me there (unless of course I'm already there.)

2. I will come over and sit in front of you (assuming I'm not already there.) I may or may not have clothes on. You'll then put

your hands on my upper legs, massaging my legs with anticipation. Keep your hands high up on my legs, massaging my legs but you may not touch my penis until allowed to.

3. I will kiss you, touch you, play with you, talk to you and undress you as you kneel submissively in front of me. At some point you may be ordered to stand up and take the rest of your clothes off. Unless you're told differently, in private, as a slave you should feel uncomfortable with clothes hiding your private parts from your Master. They exist for his pleasure afterall!

4. You will partially or fully undress me when I order you to. When you pull my pants and underwear down, you know what will pop out!

5. I will then let you suck on my penis. You will first likely have to beg for it though. Also, remember to always play with Master's testicles while you suck…always!

Rule: Never let any of Master's penis' ooze go to waste. You know good it tastes! Beg Master to let you check for ooze often! Keep sucking Master's ooze down until he allows you to stop.

6. Soon I will reach down and play with your exposed, vulnerable breasts as you suck on my penis.

7. At some point I may order you to stop sucking my penis. If so I will tie your hands securely together.

8. I may order you to suck on my penis again or we will go straight to the following:

I will sit further back on the bed (or couch/chair) and you will lay stomach down across my lap. I will give you a nice sensual spanking, playing with your body as I do.

I will then tell you to get up and we will go to the bed (if we're not already there.) I will set the bed up so I am sitting with my back against the headboard of the bed and you are laying in front of me face-down on cushions with your head positioned so you can easily suck on my penis and play with my scrotum using your tied-together hands. If I do that though I will make sure there is enough slack in the rope for your hands to still move freely around my penis and scrotum while you suck. If your hands are tied to the middle of the headboard in this manner, I will be sitting on the rope as my butt will be in-between your bound hands and the headboard which your hands are tied to.

9. I'll also put a roughly 4' x 3' (though it can be larger) sheet of plastic under your upper body to keep the massage lotion or oil from going on the bed covers. (More on this massage very soon!)

Your breasts will now be positioned, thanks to cushions, so the bottom tips (which will likely be the nipples) of the breasts are just above the bed. As you are lying down and sucking on my penis, I will **generously** lubricate (and keep lubricated,) your breasts with some brand of preferably non-desensitizing lotion or massage oil. (I prefer lotion. Baby lotions at dollar stores often are good ones to try but lotions can vary by brand.) The longer the lotion can stay viscous, the better. If warming is necessary (which it most likely will be,) I will warm the lotion/oil up ahead of time or rub it in my hands to warm it up. I will then massage your breasts as you suck on my penis and play with my testicles.

I will continue for a long time to massage your lubricated breasts as you suck on my penis. (This is known as *"Extreme Pleasure Breast Massage".*) **Remember massagers, <u>always</u> keep you're your hands well lubricated!**

Massager and massagee will quickly notice that the nipples respond with the most pleasure from this type of massage. The Dom will find that massaging his slave's breast's large fleshy area first for a while will be quite pleasurable to his slave but it is still not near as pleasurable as briskly massaging her nipples with a circular twisting motion that lets the fingers slide firmly over the nipple, not actually twisting it.

I will first make my slave beg to have her nipples massaged using this *Extreme Pleasure Breast Massage* technique. My slave has no more than 30 seconds to start her orgasm when I first start giving her *Extreme Pleasure Breast Massage*. Once I start massaging her nipples, she will have to orgasm a lot harder or risk being punished.

Using a yardstick type implement, I can also reach across your back and spank your bottom as you suck. Obviously one should make sure the woman can handle being spanked while sucking. Most can depending on the intensity of the spanking and how hard she's already orgasming.

Optional: After doing this for some time, you may wish for the lovely lady to be turned over on her back, her hands still tied to the bed. The man can then eat her. The lady should plan on providing her Master or Mistress a lot of pussy juice. Should she not provide you with enough pussy juice, feel free to turn her over so her bottom is facing up, and give her a good spanking. Then try eating her again. (Before playing it is important that the lady keep her pussy clean and fresh.) After you've had your fill of her pussy juice, both of you can go back to the original position mentioned in this section or move on to #10.

10. At some point, I may also tie each foot to its corresponding corner of the bed. Instead I may tie your feet securely together and then tie them to the middle of the bed frame at the foot of the bed. Don't worry guys, the placement of a woman's vagina on her body while she's laying on her stomach is such that you still most likely will have easy access even with her legs closed. (This could be a problem depending on how overweight she and/or he is.)

11. At some point I will order you to stop sucking by saying "head up". I will then get up and give you another spanking as you lay tied down, just for good measure. If you've been a good girl and are getting a lot of pleasure from all this, *and if you beg for it*, I will put a special vibrator (or two) inside and/or on you and set it up so it stays in place. (Tight underwear and white first aid fabric tape often works best where there are pubic hairs in the area.) I

will then return to my original position on the bed and you will continue sucking me and I will also continue giving you *Extreme Pleasure Breast Massage* (which I promise you'll enjoy immensely!) I will continue to periodically spank you with a yardstick type implement as described earlier.

12. After a while, I will order you to stop sucking. I'll then clean the lotion off your breasts with a small towel(s) and remove the small plastic sheet that caught lotion that came off your breasts and my hands. I'll also remove the cushions from under you that kept your breasts just above the bed. You are now comfortably laying face down on the bed but now without the cushions and plastic under you. You still however are tied down to the bed as you lie on your stomach. (You may wish to put a clean towel under her breasts if they are still a bit oily from the massage.) I will remove any vibrators on and/or in you, as well as whatever was holding them in place. You will be completely naked, tied down, helpless and ready to be taken.

13. I will come back in front of you and order you to suck on my penis again. After it is hard, I will dry it off and put a condom on it. I will then lay on top of you, stomach down, and enter you with my thick penis.

14. As I take you, you will orgasm for as long as I order you to and orgasm as hard as I order you to. You are <u>required,</u> as part of the orgasm on demand training, to start orgasming within 5 seconds of me entering you. Believe me it is much easier than it may sound. You will need to ask for permission to start orgasming though! As long as you start asking for permission within 5 seconds of me entering you, you are doing fine. Of course you will need permission to stop your orgasm also! There is the possibility that at some point I will order you to stop your orgasm during our lengthy playtime (or obviously you may have to do that due to unexpected events like the kids coming home early.) If you can however, you are welcome to keep orgasming even though direct sexual stimulation has temporarily stopped; (for instances after I have stopped taking you.) Once direct sexual stimulation of your breasts and your vagina restarts, you'll of course have to re-start

your orgasm once again (assuming it had stopped,) and within 5 seconds as always. (Many of the ladies I have trained will continue orgasming for many minutes after physical sexual stimulation has stopped.)

15. As I take you, you will orgasm for as long as I order you to and orgasm as hard as I order you to. Believe me young lady, I require long, hard orgasms from you.

16. As you know I am taking you while both of us are on our stomachs. My stomach of course is on your back. This is far and away the main position I will take you in for the entire time I take you. I may also take you doggie style depending on how overweight the slave is. There will however not be an emphasis on multiple sex positions during our playtime.

RULE: while I'm playing with you, if you are lying on your stomach and if I ever say "elbows" you are to raise your chest enough so that the tips of your lovely breasts are just above the bed, thus making it easier for me to play with your breasts by sliding one or more of my hands under your chest as I am taking you.

(I think you'll find that *my stomach on your back position* to be a very good one. Depending on how heavy and/or tall the guy is, you won't have any trouble breathing as my weight is well distributed over your bone-protected pelvis. You won't have to deal with my breathing on your face or you being pounded against the headboard like in the missionary position. Also I can hold you tightly as I take you and easily talk to you as my mouth can be right by your ear.

17. At some point I will slide one or both of my arms under your underarm(s) and put my hands on or around your hands. I am now securely holding you down with my hands. You can now reach my hands (as they are on your wrist, forearms or hands) and kiss them should that be our desire.

RULE: while we are playing you will only address me as "Sir" or "Master".

18. Sometimes while I am taking you like this, I will spank you. This is accomplished best by me holding myself up with one hand/arm while I am in you and then spanking you with a paddle or the like with the other hand.

19. Often I will hold you down while I take you. I will order you to struggle *FROM THE WAIST UP* to get free as I am holding you down and taking you at the same time. We will do this one or more times during our long playtime.

20. Sometimes I will take you faster than other times. You will get even more pleasure from this as most any woman would.

21. Sometimes I will thrust into you as deep and hard as I can. You will get even more pleasure from this as most any woman would.

22. This is an excellent sex position for a lady to be taken anally. Perhaps she should have her anus lubed in the beginning when she is originally laid in place incase her Master/Mistress decides to take her anally.

RULE: *Remember, the man must always wear a condom when taking her anally and he **can not** re-enter her vagina unless his pubic area has been thoroughly cleaned. A bladder infection is just one of the problems she can have if one doesn't abide by this essential safety tip.*

Remember, if something is hurting young lady, you need to tell your Master immediately so he can stop.

This book is sold and/or distributed with the understanding that the publisher and author is not engaged in rendering legal or other professional services. **This book and its subject matter is for entertainment purposes only.** In this publication there may be inadvertent inaccuracies including technical inaccuracies, typographical inaccuracies and other possible inaccuracies. **The writer and publisher of this publication expressly disclaim all liability for the use or interpretation by anybody of information contained in this publication.** The author, publisher and distributors of this publication hereby disclaim any and all liability for any loss or damage caused by errors or omissions resulted from negligence, accident, or any other causes. If legal advice or other expert assistance is required, the services of a competent professional person in a consultation capacity should be sought. Products, services and websites' content vary with time. Please verify any published information.

100 Great Lines to Put in Your Personal Ad

Introduction

The lines in this book can be combined with other lines you may think of to make your personal ad all it can be. Some lines in the book might need adapting to best suit you and/or your sex.

TAGLINES: Your short "tagline" is a headline that, perhaps along with your picture, can get readers to further explore your ad. Great taglines are like gold and people have paid hundreds of dollars for them! Now however many are on the Internet for you to see and use.

Remember, people love to laugh. A funny tagline is a big plus.

There is a great deal of material in this book to build quality taglines from. You may also want to take a bit of time and do a web search for "best personal ad taglines" for ideas. Chances are others (including those looking at your ad) haven't seen the tagline already, or have forgotten it if they did.

The Lines

It's suggested that you combine a healthy number of lines with specific information about yourself. Most of the lines below can be combined with each other so mix and match as you see fit!

A day not in love is a lost opportunity.

My friends know me as spontaneous, spritely, and upbeat.

I am searching for a beautiful person inside and out.

Are you looking for real love and someone special?

I enjoy thought provoking dialogue.

Together let's seek our destiny.

I hope only to fulfill your every desire. Is that too much to ask?
I love making people happy and to see them smile, even if at times it is at my own expense.

I feel the most pleasure when I know I am doing/enduring something to please another.

I'm looking to learn, not just to play....

I'd like to explore hidden fantasies with you.

I want to be taken to that special place and beyond.

I have the financial and emotional capacity to take care of myself.

Unlike perhaps others here I'm not misrepresenting myself. I know the importance of honesty.

I love sex. Rough sex, fun sex, emotional sex... I want you to respect me before and after but during is negotiable.

I want to explore my naughty side.

I'm looking for a friend, confidant and lover.

Like me I'd like you to be thoughtful, attractive, and looking to expand yourself as a person.

I have developed intricate pleasure techniques which can slowly arouse and pleasure beyond imagination.

I think I would describe myself, briefly, as quite a sociable person with a good sense of humor who doesn't take herself too seriously...having said that I believe I am also thoughtful and caring and someone who places great value on good friendships and relationships.

I am loyal, compassionate and respectful of people and animals. People describe me as easy going and good natured.

I have got great plans and goals in my life which I want to achieve.

I'm a contemporary yet spiritual soul in search of his charming, compassionate and caring companion to share this journey of life.

Are you looking for someone to grow with and push things further?

I have a wise mind and younger spirit.

I am an easy going, and loyal friend.

I'm looking forward to a fantastic voyage of a relationship.

I am attracted to someone who enjoys learning and growing.

Are you looking for fun, adventure and a challenge? If so I'm your girl.

I'm a passionate person with interests numerous and diverse.

I am trustworthy, affectionate, passionate, loving and non-judgmental. I am happy with myself and my accomplishments.

I want someone kind, loving, honest, communicative and self-aware. Your developed interest in education, hygiene, aesthetics, style and emotional literacy would make life easier for us. I'd like to find someone interested in building a relationship based on an accomplished life and a win/win attitude.

I am looking for someone who can work themselves deep inside my mind and make me fall to my knees.

Are you looking for someone to make you happy...someone that won't just have sex with you but will make love to you?

We all want to achieve heart pounding serenity.

I am looking for something more than just sex and games. Sure sex is a part of it but I also want someone that I can spend time with. I want the total package.

I want someone that I can go out with, talk with, laugh with, and fall in love with.

Outside of our playtime, I'd like to enjoy a harmony that can grow into a loving, trusting relationship. I enjoy the outdoors and staying healthy, going out on the town from time to time and hanging out at home.

My last relationship ended because we grew in different directions.

I am usually lucky and love life. I would like to find someone like that.

I'm a strong, seductive, passionate woman who is established and knows herself.

I'm well educated and well-travelled. I'm gainfully employed and very independent. I enjoy traveling, good food and wine, the theater and sports.

I'm searching for an open minded man with an adventurous soul and sensual heart. A journey in love is the destination. We still have plenty of time but none to waste! A beautiful world is waiting. Let's enjoy while we can!

I'll laugh at your corny jokes.

I'm a writer and voracious reader. I'm smart, and I like smart people.

Physical attraction leads to animal instincts.

I have a strong passion for the exploration and power of touch in all its forms.
I enjoy knowledge, I like to learn new and exciting things.

I am cosmopolitan and highly educated. I am a baby boomer, in good shape and would like an agemate and a partner who understands mutuality. I am interested in developing a long term relationship.

I am interested in meeting someone who is honest, open and enjoys (his)her kink.

I have very many interests and I'm passionate about all of them! I love movies, literature, music, art, theatre, science... and lots of other things.

I am fun, open-minded, spontaneous and down for raunchy action.

The reason openness is important to me is that it shows that someone accepts themselves.

I'm lively and active and have a well developed sense of humor.

I hope to always be me and take advantage of any opportunities and chances whenever they're thrown at me.

I am totally devoted when in love.

I'm a laid-back, drama-free kind of person.

I want to be late to my own funeral.

Physical play is quite enjoyable but chemistry and a connection is more important.

I like to laugh, I like to have fun.

I believe that love is not what we see but what we do.

I won't ignore you or abandon you. I'm not looking for a secondary relationship.

I have a well developed and dominant sexual identity. I am seeking a man who is a smart, uninhibited, challenging partner.

I consider myself a natural leader, an innovator, a creator. I fight for the best and readily take the risks incumbent with leading a fulfilled, enriched life.

I am a strong, confident thinker, with a secure sense of himself (herself).

I consider myself to be a spontaneous, fun loving person. I work hard, play hard, and enjoy life. I'm a very affectionate and passionate. I like to hold hands and believe it or not cuddle. I believe in treating others the way I would like to be treated. I am looking for someone to grow with spiritually, mentally and physically. I want someone who is not afraid to love and be loved, someone who is affectionate, passionate and good kisser.

I will love you and take good care of you. I am someone who you can trust and believe in, someone who will always want to make you feel happy.

I'm neat and clean both internally and externally.

I want true love and real commitment.

I am looking for something more than just sex and games. There is a balance that is needed since none of us can live in a purely sexual world. Sure sex is an important part of it all but I also want someone that I can spend time with. I want the total package. I want someone I can go out with, talk with, laugh with, and fall in love with.

I want something that will naturally grow and evolve into its own very beautiful story.

I enjoy a great number of things and am very open to experimentation.
I'm interested in your fantasies.

I want to touch your body, your soul, your life.

I still believe that fairytales can come true, it can happen to us...

I live a healthy lifestyle. I am seeking the same.

I am brimming with sexual desire.

I will be looking forward to hear from you and Your wish will always be done...

I am looking for a partner - but I am happy to form a friendship.

Living on earth is expensive...but it does include free trips around the sun.

I eat healthy and workout regularly.

I am an educated, intelligent professional with eclectic tastes in most everything: art, music, food, people, entertainment and travel.

I'm looking for a non-smoker to share my life with in all ways, a friend and companion to travel with, commiserate over bad days and rejoice over good days; a lover and confidant.

Educated, professional and kinky.

I have class and style. I know the value of dressing to impress.

I would love to be able to say "I've finally found you."

I believe that we all have the ability to create or change anything.

I consider myself to be a sharp, crafty, inventive, fun, strong woman who enjoys life more when she's in a relationship.

I'm looking for a like minded man to chat, debate and play with.

I'm not a just fantasist wasting your time.

I am people biased not gender biased.

I am family-oriented and have family values.

I possess confidence but take pride in not being arrogant. I'm persistent but respectful. I have intelligence and charm.

I don't like negative people. We're here to live life not fear it.

I have learned in life that the smallest good deed is better than the grandest good intention.

I have high hopes for us.

I am a sharp, crafty, inventive, fun woman who doesn't hate men or hate anyone for that matter.

I enjoy life so much more when I'm in a relationship.

What you are like OUT of bed makes you more desirable for me to want you to take me there.

I like to please as much as be pleased.

I want to discover and explore my limits as well as push them further.

I like intellectual conversations.

My ambition is self-actualisation, to release the potential within.

I'm thoughtful, devoted, industrious, competitive, genuine and trustworthy.

I'm looking to learn and grow, not just to play....